TAMING TIME

TAMING TIME

the Small Business Owner's Guide to More Time, Money, and Fun

Shauna E. VanderHoek

Copyright © Shauna E VanderHoek, 2018

All rights reserved. No part of this book may be reproduced or transmitted in any form or by any means, mechanical or electronic, including photocopying or recording, or by any information storage and retrieval system, or transmitted by email without permission in writing from the author.

Reviewers may quote brief passages in reviews.

First Edition: May 2018
ISBN: 978-1-7323483-1-8

Published by Good Biz Choice Press
Sarasota, Florida, USA

Dedication

This book is dedicated to you, the small business owner, someone who knows you can make a difference and wants to have fun and be profitable along the way.

This book is also dedicated to my son, who aspires to have his own business.

Creating a business is a journey,
but that's part of the fun!

Table of Contents

Introduction — 1
    The Crash and Starting Over — 1
    I Have a Dream — 3
    It's Time for You to Have Your Dream — 5

The Problem — 9
    Margaret's Struggle — 9
    Big Challenges — 12
    The "Business is Great!" Lie — 13
    Exercise: The 3 Magic Steps — 14
    One Business Owner's Success — 21
    In Summary — 22

Mindset — 23
    Debra's Glass Ceiling — 23
    Conscious or Unconscious? — 25
    Exercise: "What's Stopping Me?" — 27
    The Five Steps—a Recap — 35
    Mindset Shapes Attitude — 36

What Do You Want?	**38**
Waiting for the Morning	38
Do You Really Want More?	41
Exercise: Define/Refine Your Dream	43
In Summary	52
Having Fun?	**54**
Business Is No Fun Anymore	54
My Toughest Lesson: Fun	55
Fun Is Subjective	56
The Fun of Doing	57
Fun During a Business Day	57
Exercise: How to Expand the Fun Factor	59
Overcome Overwhelm	**68**
Overwhelm Can Kill	68
Three Steps Out Of Overwhelm	69
To Summarize the Three Step Solution	78
Twenty-four Hours a Day	**80**
My Journey With Time	80
The First Truth of Time	82
Not all at Once!	83
"Right Now!" Priorities	84

Quick Tips to spend your 24 hours more wisely.	87
Details That Save You	89
Time Is For Sale	**92**
The Second Truth of Time:	92
5 Easy Steps To Systematize Repetitive Processes	94
You're Hired!	98
The Price and Benefits	99
Personal Time	**102**
No Respect	102
The Third Truth of Time	104
Learn to say No	106
Time Hides	**110**
The Fourth Truth of Time	110
The Internet	110
Interrupted vs. In The Groove	114
Chores: Who does them?	114
Time Blocking	115
Time is Like a Lover	**118**
The Fifth Truth of Time	118
Unplugged	119

Self-Care: Preparing Yourself for Your Lover   120
The Five Truths of Time—a Recap   123

Next Steps   **124**
Pattern Change   124
Simple Pattern-Change Tips   125
It Takes a Village...   129
Time to Thrive!   131

Acknowledgments   **134**

About the Author   **136**

Free Bonus!   **140**

Introduction

The Crash and Starting Over

Remember the dot-com crash of 2001? Many people lost heaps of money, sometimes their entire retirement accounts, investing in the promise of technology. When the crash happened, IT (Internet Technology) consultants were the first ones laid off, soon followed by layoffs of tens of thousands of employees.

One of my peers went from earning six figures to taking a job for $25,000 per year. Me? Once an IT consultant, I worked as a bartender in a neighborhood dive bar and made even less.

Coming back from the collapse made me doubly determined to leave IT and share my 25 years of business knowledge with other small business owners.

Why should they go through some of the pain I've dealt with?

But the Universe wasn't done with me yet. I knew I wanted to "help" but wasn't clear on how to roll my knowledge out to people who needed me. As soon as I found a new IT client and had my feet underneath me, I worked "two jobs"—my daytime IT contract, and planning my new business. The latter consumed my evenings and weekends.

The IT Consulting industry, for independents like me, never really recovered. Time between contracts grew longer. The new international market, consultants from overseas, undercut prices; I could no longer receive the rate I previously earned. Between contracts I worked on the new business, but never launched it for fear of failure (another lesson learned).

Five years into this rollercoaster of income, no income, and vagueness about my new business, I had my legs cut out from me once again. I was only six weeks into a one year contract at Chico's, just pulling out of the red, when a new CIO terminated all consultants company-wide—effective immediately—while she reevaluated expenses.

Emotionally, physically, and financially drained, I hit adrenal burnout. Adrenals help control the heart, kidneys, and immune system. Adrenal burnout results in a fatigue that you can't seem to shake, sleep that eludes you, body aches, digestive problems, and shattered nerves.

My years of living in stress had taken its toll. It was no fun! I could barely function.

I reached out for help. A friend recommended a not-so-typical coach, a business woman who looked not only at my work-driven habits. She took me deeper to reveal what was behind my personal patterns.

As the song says, it takes a while to turn the Titanic around, and I did. Now I have clients I love, a consistent income, time for myself, a new relationship … and I am more at peace and having more fun than ever before.

I Have a Dream

I have a dream. I believe small businesses—entrepreneurs, small firms, and self-employed persons—are the key to the success of our economy.

Even while I was working with companies like Apple and AT&T to manage their multimillion dollar projects and streamline their business systems, I hung out at seminars and conferences for small business owners. I fell in love with the entrepreneurial spirit. They are the under-acknowledged contributors, the innovation engine of our future. Small businesses owners have the potential to make a huge difference on our planet.

It's not only me who thinks so. According to the Small Business Administration,

- Small businesses (firms with 1-499 employees) continue to add more net new jobs than large businesses (500+ employees)
- Firms with less than 20 workers made up 89.4 percent of businesses and added 1.1 million net jobs in 2015.
- Micro-businesses (less than 5 employees) collectively contribute over $1 trillion in earnings to the economy.

Heifer International (my favorite charity, founded in 1944) thinks highly of small businesses owners as well. They helped 30 million families in more than 125 countries—including the United States—improve their quality of life and move toward greater self-reliance. They say "We have learned the most reliable, sustainable way to end hunger and poverty is to develop and strengthen local economies."

When business owners are financially successful, it contributes to economic growth, increases consumption, improves public services, and reduces unemployment and poverty.

When people are doing work they love, contributing their talents and fulfilling their personal dreams, it breeds increased happiness which in turn inspires peace.

I'm all about peace, free enterprise, and success. It's why I am passionate about small businesses owners. Small business is the future of this country.

It's Time for You to Have Your Dream

This book gives you tools and exercises to keep you on course during your personal journey Taming Time. Working with these tools will allow you to breathe, not just for a moment before the next sprint, the next crush of too much to do, but in the midst of the crush.

As the saying goes, life is what you make it. The exercises in this book are designed to help you have more time, money, and fun in both your business and your life. It's possible. This book shows you how.

Enjoy!
Shauna

Chapter 1

The Problem

Margaret's Struggle

Margaret restlessly tossed and turned. It was 1 AM, and she could not fall asleep. She had taken time from her business in the afternoon for a conference with her daughter's high school counselor. Now her mind was in overdrive from sitting in front of her computer to make up the lost time.

Lately, it seemed evenings were the only time she could work on her business. It was getting old.

Her daughter Cindy walked by a couple of times as she worked this evening, probably to further the conversation about going to college. Margaret felt terrible for not taking a break from work to see what she needed, but how could she send Cindy to college unless something changed with her business, and soon.

Frank, her ex-husband, said he couldn't afford to help with Cindy's college. He stopped paying child support in February when Cindy turned eighteen. Meanwhile, he was spending his money taking his latest squeeze on weekend getaways. Rumor had it they were planning a two-week trip to Paris in the fall.

"Life is so not fair," Margaret muttered as she gave up on sleep, pulled on a robe, and sat back down in front of the computer. But instead of working she stared at her screen. She couldn't get her mind off Cindy. They had made it through the early teens and had a pretty decent relationship, but if she couldn't even take time from work to talk with her…

Margaret had high hopes for her business. It was finally taking off when Frank walked out 18 months ago. What looked like good money for a two-income household was barely enough to scrape by.

Margaret sat back and thought of what things could be like if she had more time, more money coming in. She could be there for her daughter. Heck, she could be there for herself! The beach was only ten miles away, but it had been six weeks since she last took a walk and felt the warm sand between her toes. She had her nails done professionally for a put together look at networking events, but she couldn't remember her last spa day.

Too tired to focus well enough to accomplish any real work, she grabbed a cup of tea and sat down with her journal. "Visualizing will help me clear my mind," she thought. After all, sports figures claimed to win by visualizing the ball dropping through the hoop before they take their shot.

Margaret jotted down a list of what she might visualize. "Time for leisure," she wrote, then shook her head. "Not going to happen. I need to be working more, not taking time off."

"More money in less time—Ha, like that can happen! Maybe I should find a part-time job. At least I would have some money I could count on." But she knew this was not the answer.

"Make a bigger difference for my clients."

"Helping make a difference with my clients would feel good, but I already over deliver for what I am paid," she thought. How could she give more? She was already stretched thin.

Frustrated, Margaret headed back to bed to finish out a night of restless sleep.

Big Challenges

In a Forbes article, John Hall reported the most significant challenges facing fast-growing companies. These were challenges Margaret faced. As a small businesses owner, maybe you face some of these too.

- Keeping your family happy and continually deciding when to miss important family events because of work demands.
- Trying to wear too many hats instead of hiring the people you need and getting them productive, fast
- Losing track of the big picture; stuck in the daily grind

I've been up against all these same problems. I lost everything when the dot.com industry crashed in 2001—including my client base (a perfect example of putting all your eggs in one basket and expecting it to last forever).

The "Business is Great!" Lie

Does this sound familiar?

"Hey Nicole, how's business?"

"It's great! My new program is a hit."

Like you will tell them anything else... Your new program was a hit, but the profits? What profits? After the cost of the web design, the extra work your Virtual Assistant had to put in, all the money you paid for coaching, your internet and utility bills, and the after-school care for your child so you could work longer hours, the profits disappeared faster than a toupee in a hurricane.

Lack of profits is fine ...if all you want is to spread the word, do the work you love, and make a difference. Those things matter. But is it enough?

There is nothing wrong with "fine." According to the Oxford Dictionary, it means things are good, satisfactory, pleasing. Maybe "fine" is enough for you.

But what if, instead of fine, you want your business, your life, to be more? What if it could be fantastic? What if you could make more money, have more time, and reach a bigger audience?

If your business isn't as fantastic as you want it to be, you might recognize these symptoms:

- Your business is no fun anymore.
- You know it's time to hire someone, but looks like more work than it is worth.
- There is not enough time to stop and smell the roses.
- Your family is complaining.
- You're complaining! ...and you still aren't bringing in the money you want.

I can relate. I've been in all of those spots and then some. It's a terrible place to be.

Exercise: The 3 Magic Steps

If you want more, if you are asking, "Now what?" here are Three Magic Steps to transform your business as well as your relationships, your health, and your finances. These three steps can transform "Fine" into "Fantastic."

I will give you all three steps at once, at the risk of you saying, "Duh. As if I didn't know that!" But don't let their simplicity fool you. The "secret sauce" is in truly understanding what goes behind each of the steps But first, the big-picture:

1. Identify the problem.
2. Decide what YOU really want.
3. Design and implement a solution.

OK, OK! Obvious? Yes, you think you know what the problem is. Yes, you may be clear on what you want.

But you probably wouldn't be reading this unless you have problems with Step 3. And you can't arrive at Step 3 if you don't complete Steps 1 and 2 correctly.

Step One: Identify the problem.

I headed to the airport for an early morning flight to a business conference. It was still dark out, but I live in a well-lit neighborhood. I drove on the equally well-lit main roads and was thinking: "I really need to have my eyes checked. I think my night vision is getting worse."

A few miles later, I see those red and blue flashing lights in the lane behind me. I looked at my speedometer. Drat! I was going almost 50 mph in a 45 mph zone. I pulled off into a parking lot and opened the window. I believe "innocent until proven guilty" and always be courteous, so I asked, "How can I help you, officer?"

Her response surprised me. She said, "Do you realize you have no headlights?" Since my mechanic fixed a brake light a week earlier (and checked all my lights and assured me everything was working), it never occurred to me the headlights—not night blindness—was the problem.

Sometimes what we think is the problem is merely a symptom. Sometimes we are too close to the problem to see it clearly. Sometimes we need an outside perspective.

Identifying the real problem is one reason coaches have coaches. It's why masterminds are so helpful. It is also why companies like Apple and Winn-Dixie hire people like me: I typically uncover deeper problems lurking beneath the surface. There are usually entire business workflows requiring attention before the company can achieve the success they want.

An outside perspective is valuable. Others can see things you are too close to see. Even talking to a good friend who can be objective will give you a powerful step up in helping identify the real problem.

> Step One: Know what
> the problem is.

Step Two: Decide what YOU really want.

This step is near and dear to my heart. I spent nearly eight years in between corporate contracts trying to figure out what was next. I knew I wanted to share my business knowledge and experience with small businesses owners, but how? So I took a lot of courses, went to a lot of trainings, and worked with a lot of well-meaning coaches.

I learned a great deal and received many great ideas. But many of those ideas derailed me from my original vision. I heard a lot of "you can't do that, you should this, you should that." Some of it was bigger than I wanted to do; some of it was too small to suit me.

Problems are not **stop signs**. They are **guidelines**.

Robert Schuller

I finally had to throw away other people's shoulds and set my own course. I even had to throw away various stories and rules from when I grew up. Stories like "you have to work 40-60 hours a week to be a success." Rules like "You have to work hard just to get by."

Get back in touch with your vision. What's the end game you really want?

Whose rules are you following? Whose expectations are you trying to live up to? Who are you trying to not disappoint by making the decision you want to make? Forget about what other people think. You are the one who decides: what do YOU really want?

A friend recently talked to me about designing my life. He mentioned Babe Ruth. Remember the name from the Baseball Hall of Fame? He earned the nickname "Home Run King" by setting a record of more than 714 home runs during his 22 years in the major leagues. His success is an excellent example of successful execution of all three steps:

1. Babe Ruth identified the problem: he loved baseball, but he was slow and fat. Out-racing

the ball to the next base wasn't going to work for him.

2. He became clear on what was most important to him. He REALLY wanted to play baseball. And he didn't want to lose weight or hurry up. (Knowing what you don't want is as important as knowing what you do want.)

Which leads us to...

Step Three: Design and implement a solution.

Create and execute the plan to develop the time, money and fun you want and deserve. Unfortunately, most people try to design and implement a solution before they've completed steps one and two: identify the real problem and, more importantly, decide what they truly want for themselves.

Back to Babe Ruth, who implemented a solution turning him into the Home-Run King. His Step Three was:

> With every swing,
> go for the home run.

With a home run Babe could do a slow jog around the bases. (No having to lose weight, no having to hurry.) He implemented and succeeded in his solution. Babe held the home-run record for 39 years.

Solutions can be clear-cut (like focus on connecting the bat to the ball to get a home run) or complex (like the six-to-eighteen-month project plans I develop for large corporations). I love designing and implementing solutions. To do this step justice here would take another entire book. We dive into it more deeply in the *Time to Thrive* program.

One Business Owner's Success

A few years ago the owner of a small acupuncture practice asked me to work with her. Dr. Rose. was working too hard and not making the income she expected. Lack of income was the symptom.

I guided her through the three steps to reveal her solution.

Step 1: Identify the problem.
In short order, we identified two areas in her business to make the most significant impact: her team and her marketing.

Step 2: What did she want?
More time and a better income.

Step 3: What is the solution?
I walked her through my hiring system, and we quickly found an awesome assistant. At the same time, we tweaked the structure and strategy behind her newsletter.

The result? We doubled her revenues in less than 90 days.

In Summary

If you want to go from Fine to Fantastic, follow the three magic steps.

- Identify the problem.
- Decide what you really want.
- Design and implement a solution.

Designing a solution is a favorite segment in the program, *Time to Thrive*. We create a complete roadmap to guide you through the steps from where you are to where you want to be.

Chapter 2

Mindset

Debra's Glass Ceiling

Debra looked back at her business income for the past eight months and asked, "How could I have been so blind?"

The April 15th tax deadline was fast approaching. She pulled together the numbers for her prior business year and expected them to be a bit light. She had great clients but had put others on hold while she helped her new boyfriend launch his business. (Of course! She was in love.)

"This can't be right," Debra mumbled as she checked last year's income one more time. She had taken three months off from her business—conducting training for larger companies—but she made the same amount she had made every year for the past four years.

Debra thought back. A new client had hired her early in the year to support their fast-growing company's Human Resources department. They offered her the best rate she'd ever received (nearly 150% of what she usually charged) but required her to travel half-way across the country, back and forth every week, to corporate headquarters. Six months into the contract, she decided she didn't want to travel so much. How weird, because she loved to travel.

A voice in her head argued: "They put you up in the Marriott. You ate fine dining every night on their budget." It was true, but Debra didn't want to do it anymore, so she found a good stopping place in the contract and gave notice.

Looking back as she pulled her tax information together, Debra recognized the truth: she hit her glass ceiling (the unofficial, invisible barrier to better wages and career advancement). Even though she hadn't tracked her year to date income, she stopped working once her year reached a certain level of income.

Debra had a hidden mindset and called on me to help identify it. After working together, she realized she earned what her parents made, combined. She was not allowing herself to earn any more. This false sense of loyalty sabotaged her income for years. The following year she raised her income by 25%.

Yes, there is a glass ceiling, and "they" (the old boys' network) are not the problem!

Debra's story is one example of how mind sabotage shows up. Some people immigrate to a new country with a dream and make it come true, while others wish, hope, complain, and allow themselves only a meager portion of what's available. Is it because they can't see themselves worthy of "having" more than what they now have? Or do they subconsciously dare not earn more than their parents did out of a false sense of allegiance?

Conscious or Unconscious?

I remember my first major financial breakthrough.

My career was doing fine. One weekend I went to a meditation retreat. It wasn't the normal sit-and-make-your-mind-go-blank kind of meditation. (Uh-uh. Can't do those!) With these guided meditations you go into your past and into your subconscious to explore pivotal moments where you first formed a belief or simply accepted one handed to you.

What I found during the retreat changed my life and my sense of self-worth. I recalled an incident where, as a toddler, my sister (as children will do) went on a mad tirade about something. I was barely old enough to understand words, but from the energetic blast, I received a message saying I was no better than a piece of garbage. Since she was older, she must be wiser, right? Fast-forward twenty years and I was still carrying the debilitating belief in my unconscious.

Once the belief became conscious, I could see it as false and let it go. Within ten days following the retreat—without even reaching out to any companies—a new client offered a contract at 30% more than my top rate. Within weeks after taking on the contract, they asked me to manage a multimillion-dollar project. I had more fun with this project than I'd ever had in business—and it wasn't the money!

A few years later, I more than doubled my rate again ... all because I found and removed a sabotaging belief of my sense of self-worth, one that did not serve me or the life I wanted.

Beliefs are thoughts you keep thinking. Limiting beliefs are nothing more than Stinking Thinking—thoughts to sabotage your ability to have the life you want. Recognizing your Stinking Thinking is the only way you can change.

Your mindset, which consists of your beliefs and attitude, is the foundation on which you build—or sabotage—your success, your fun, and your freedom.

Exercise: "What's Stopping Me?"

Let's look at where you are right now. There is something you need to accomplish, but you aren't able to complete the task. Why not? Walking through the five steps will help you find the answer to the question.

Step 1: What do you need to accomplish "right now?"

Think of something you must do today or this week, something you don't have time for, or you feel you don't have enough time to do it right. Is it something promised to a client or family member, bills to pay, or a long overdue change to your website?

What do you need to do right now? Pick something. (You gain more value from this chapter, this book, if you play along.) OK. Next.

Step 2: Observe and rate the feeling.

Hold the challenge in mind and check in with your body. Where are you holding the stress? On a scale of 1 to 10, how uncomfortable or painful is it? There is nothing to do about it right now. Simply observe.

Let me digress for a moment and tell you about a study completed between 1924 and 1932 at the Hawthorne Works near Chicago. The company wanted to know if the level of light in their building affected the productivity of the workers. Interestingly enough, productivity improved no matter whether the amount of light increased or decreased.

The workers increased output because they were aware they were under observation. In quantum mechanics, the observer and what is being observed are mysteriously linked. People, situations, and things can change under observation. The Hawthorne Works story shows the impact of simple observation, something you can use to your advantage.

For now, notice and observe your responses.

Step 3: Identify the belief behind the feeling.

Ask yourself: "What do I believe about this situation to make me feel stressed?"

I used this process recently when facing a client deadline. They wanted me notify them by the end of day Friday about a major project they would consider, but only if I could complete it within eight months. To give them an answer, I would need to flesh out all the detailed steps and make sure the right people could commit to the planned dates. One person in the domino chain effect could derail the whole timeline.

"How could one person derail a timeline?" you ask. Take the example of putting up a new website. Maybe you've lived this experience. It wouldn't matter if your web designer could put the site up tomorrow if you can't hand her the copy, the graphics, and the overall layout. The web designer is downstream in the

Once your **mindset** changes, **everything on the outside** will change along with it.

Steve Maraboli

row of dominos. If the designer does not know exactly what you want, if the person writing the copy or the person designing any special graphics can't hand their part off, the web designer cannot complete the project on schedule.

Back to the question for step three: "What do I believe about this situation to make me feel stressed?" I only had three days to design a project expected to take eight months.

My first answer, my initial reaction or belief, was "I will never complete this on time." A rather general response, so I drilled deeper. "There are too many moving parts; I don't have time to complete the plan, identify all the players (the 'dominos'), and check in with them to make sure they can commit before I hand this over to my client." My fear was valid.

Step 4: Is this belief valid?

Next question: "This thing I believe, is it absolutely true?"

In the case of my client's Friday deadline and all the people I would need to touch base with, maybe it was true. Maybe not. Perhaps I could get in touch with some of them, or none or all. The good news is often the very act of identifying what's troubling you will allow you to do one of three things:

1. Toss it out as a needless worry (not the case here!)
2. Use the information to solve that problem (knowing what you are up against can be very motivating)
3. Set it to one side and work on the pieces you can control.

In my client deadline scenario, I took option C. Now I knew what my worries were; I could focus on laying out the rest of the plan with reasonable time estimates for each step.

I completed the detailed plan quickly, since I wasn't dragging the extra worry around with me and could receive commitments from 60% of the people involved. My client received a quick answer and was okay with the caveat about the missing time commitments. They decided to go ahead with the project.

Step 5. Is it hurting or helping?

If step four did not shift your mind and set it at ease, ask yourself the next question:

Is this belief hurting or serving me?

This one is tricky. If you will stop and acknowledge how this belief is hurting you, it can create the very motivation to change the same belief. Likewise, acknowledging your belief is serving you, even if the belief itself appears to be hurtful, can be an empowering step.

I experienced this consciously for the first time when I was working through some relationship issues with a caring and intuitive life coach. Based on experience, I had decided men weren't safe. I wanted to be in a relationship again, so this belief, or decision, was definitely in the way, but some part of me wasn't willing to release it.

My coach asked, "How is this belief serving you?"

The answer came quickly: "I'm more cautious when I date. I try to find out the kind of person they are before I meet them. We meet in a safe place with people around. I don't give a guy my address until we've gone out a few times."

Wow! I realized this "negative" belief was actually serving me!

Since then, I've grown and let that across-the-board, limiting belief go. I still keep up with the safe dating practices, but I now have way more fun on my dates.

The Five Steps—a Recap

Keep these handy. Use them whenever you find yourself stopped.

1. What do you need to accomplish "right now"?
2. Observe and rate the feeling.
3. Identify the belief behind the feeling.
4. Is the belief valid?
5. Is it hurting or helping?

In business, you may think (i.e., believe) you can't accomplish what's needed in time. It could be true or it could be false. When you identify the belief behind the thought (decision), and identify whether the thought hurts or helps, then you can move forward in making the right decisions. What you uncover can serve you to take the right action, e.g., grow your team, cut your commitments, or both.

If it's a limiting belief you are operating from, remember: a belief is a mindset you have repeated so often it becomes entrenched. If what you believe isn't working for you anymore, it's a signpost something needs to change.

Caution: There are people who claim their debilitating beliefs as true and immovable. They wield their "truth" to hang onto a sense of victimhood and excuse their lack of action. If you meet up with these people, step away. They will only drag you down.

Mindset Shapes Attitude

Some say mindset is a set of attitudes. Others say your mindset shapes your attitude, which your attitude reinforces your mindset.

Dictionary.com describes mindset as "A fixed mental attitude or disposition that predetermines a person's responses to and interpretations of situations." They describe attitude as "manner, disposition, feeling, position, etc., with regard to a person or thing; tendency or orientation, especially of the mind." Oxford Dictionary says, "Mindset is the established set of attitudes held by someone." Ash Buchanan, designer and founder of Benefit Mindset, says, "Mindsets shape the lives we lead, the actions we take and the future possibilities of the shared world we live in."

Like the chicken and the egg, it doesn't matter which came first. Mindset and attitude go hand in hand.

Mindset is your magic wand.

Chapter 3

What Do You Want?

Waiting for the Morning

It was 3:30 a.m. I was awake. Poised for action, but there was nothing to do. Okay, there was plenty to do, but now wasn't the time. Any sensible person sleeps at this hour. Besides, the warmth of the covers made me snuggle further down in my bed.

So I lay there, waiting.

Waiting for what? Maybe I could sleep if I knew the answer. Just knowing might put my mind at ease. My body was tense, on alert for a signal to tell me what to do next.

Underneath it all, this was how I was living my life. Waiting. Distracting myself with things like my "day job" (current full-time contract), paying the bills, taking care of the house, the occasional outing with friends.

I had no sense of direction. I was filling time.

Sure, I had hopes and dreams. I had some great ideas for a business I could start. Anything would be more fulfilling than my current day job. But I couldn't seem to get moving on them. I wanted a relationship but had been single for so long I had pretty much given up ... and was doing nothing about it.

I was waiting. Poised for action and going nowhere. Were my adrenals shot because of this constant, underlying "fight-or-flight" tension?

There are all kinds of "WAITING."

One kind is where you are about to walk through a doorway and the person ahead of you stops, holds up a hand, and says "wait." Your forward momentum stops. It's a state of limbo. It's likely to be a short wait, but you don't know, once the wait is over, what will happen. Will you be able to move forward? Will you have to retreat? Take a step back? Or will it turn into a longer wait?

Suppose it's the longer wait, a stressful wait. You are waiting on outside circumstances. This can take place in an emergency waiting room, not knowing what news you might receive while the doctor examines the injury—or multiple injuries—of a loved one. Or it could be in the waiting room upstairs in the same building, pacing while your wife/daughter/sister goes into her ninth hour of labor (a hopeful event, but stressful). Or you may wait in your own home, worried because your teenager didn't come home last night.

Sometimes, waiting can instill a sense of positive excitement. Like being all packed for vacation hours or days before you need to leave. Or waiting can carry an element of dread, like having your home and dinner prepared well before your oh-so-judgmental in-laws arrive—late, as usual.

Waiting can cause stress, fill you with hope, or both—like waiting for the birth of a child. It can give a sense of going nowhere, weighing your spirit down.

It can be like hitting the pause button ("Wait!") on one thing to allow time for something else. The wait could be small: While I waited for the internet to come back online, I filed the stack of papers that had been … waiting.

The wait could be significant. During an extended power outage during Hurricane Irma (really extended!—it took several days before they restored the power), I turned on my solar-powered camping lantern and reorganized my closet, read a book, and painted my toenails.

But no, in this case, I was "waiting for the morning." (Don't you hate the waiting during a sleepless night as you lie in bed?) Maybe it was time to figure out what I wanted in the "morning." How did I want my life to look and feel five or ten years from now?

There had to be something more, something other than the life I was living. It was time to figure it out.

Do You Really Want More?

Scott Dinsmore, Founder of Live Your Legend, said,

"The curse of too much is everywhere:

- We think we need more food than we do so we overeat.

- We think we need more space than we do so we buy too big a home.
- We think we need more things than we do so we overspend.
- We think we need more money than we do so we overwork.
- We think we need more freedom than we do so we end up alone."

In his article, *The Curse of Too Much: Why Most People Never Live Their Dreams and What to Do About It*[1], he says, "Define your dreams." Let's talk about them.

If you already have a business, at some point (however vaguely), you defined your dreams. Stop for a moment now and bring your dream to mind: What is your business dream?

Perhaps you want to be your own boss, pay the bills, have a bit of freedom. Maybe your dream is to have a team to run your business while you travel the world. Maybe you even planned and are on track, for a six, seven, or eight-figure business. Or your dream could be "Get my message out" or "Save the planet."

---

[1] Go to www.askShauna.com/BONUS for links and resources and more.

Dinsmore's first step is excellent, by itself, for someone starting in business. But for those of us already trucking down the "live your dream—own a business" path, he missed a few pieces to ensure this is the "right" dream to have a satisfying business.

Do this exercise now to fill in the missing steps:

Exercise: Define/Refine Your Dream

Here are four questions to clarify and refine—and maybe redefine—your dream. Who you were then is not who you are now.

1. How have you defined your dream so far?

For the existing business owners, you have a dream you've been working toward. This same dream currently has you feeling overwhelmed, discouraged, or frustrated (the reason you are reading this book).

Here is a critical step: Write down how you currently define your dream. This can be an eye-opener.

2. Do you still want the same dream? If not, then What?

You've heard of Isaac Newton, yes? Newton's First Law states an object will remain at rest or "in uniform motion in a straight line" (i.e., it will keep doing what it's been doing) unless acted upon by an external force.

This step is essential to having a satisfying business. This step is the external force to "act upon" what is not working and allow you to change course if needed. Or it could give you the extra push to increase your momentum and accelerate your results. It's the check-up to make sure you have Step 1 locked and loaded before going any further.

Sometimes we start with a vision of what our business could/should be. We may even find some measure of success, but it's not enough. We want more. Sometimes we think we want more of the wrong thing, like money.

For example, my friend Jane. Several years into her successful, multi-six-figure business, she became bored. She was disenchanted with her business. Yes, she loved making a difference, she enjoyed her clients,

If you don't know
where you are going,
any road
will get you there.

Lewis Carroll

but the rest of it wasn't working. Until she could admit she did not still want the same dream which brought her here, she remained stuck.

It turns out she didn't want "more"—she wanted less! Fortunately, she redefined her dream and is now making even more money working fewer hours, and is happier than she had been in years. (Which proves the adage, "Less is more" … if you have the right "What.")

Ultimately we all want happiness. Everything we do is an effort to get there—the car we choose, where we live, the fights we pick, the friends we hang out with, and the business we launch.

Do you really want your current "dream" if it is giving you so much trouble?

If you are still saying "Yes" to your dream—even though it has been costing you sleep and causing your pain—it is time to find out why.

I wish I could stop right here and spend a day with you to drill into this. (We go deep in the Pleasure Planning segment of *Time to Thrive*. After all, if your business isn't fun, isn't pleasurable, why bother?) Here, in a nutshell, are the first few steps:

- Imagine each element of the business you want.
- Take a look at each one and ask: "How does this feel? Does it make me light up?"
- Note what feels good; note what doesn't feel quite so good (or downright awful).
- Decide what needs to change.

If none of the elements of your business feel right, it might be time to scrap this dream and build a new one. If it's a mixed bag, focus on the good elements, the ones that inspire you. Narrowing your dream down to what works for you and eliminating what doesn't will allow you to move past stuck and live your dream.

3. Is it yours?

This is critical—more so because it is easily overlooked. Examine your dream and where it began. Was this dream handed to you by parents or a well-meaning relative? Did it latch into your mind based on a long forgotten comment from an authority figure? If you try to live the dream others say you "should" want, it will only wear you out. No more!

If you find it originated with someone else, it's time to sing the 60's Animals' song, "It's my life and I'll do what I want." Make sure your dream is your own and not imposed by an outside force. Miss this step and you risk wasting precious time and energy.

4. Why do you want it?

We talked about What. It speaks to where are you going, what will it look like when you arrive. Almost more important than the What is the WHY, i.e., your purpose. Purpose (sometimes called Mission) is not the same as the What, the goal. Your Purpose is personal. It's the reason behind the dream; it's the reason the dream even exists. It's the feeling, the end-game you hope to achieve.

Take Greg. He had a successful online business selling car parts. Ever since he was a kid, he was crazy about cars: driving them, tinkering with them, rebuilding them, and sometimes racing them. The parts business gave him an excuse to go where other car enthusiasts hung out—NASCAR Races, Exotic Car Festivals,

Automotive Parts Conventions, and various car shows and events.

It provided a good living but cost him more time than he wanted to give. He was thinking of partnering up with someone to take on more of the technical stuff—website upkeep, posting new parts, price changes, page rankings—but it would be up to Greg to negotiate the wholesale deals to keep the profit margins up.

Greg was waiting to decide. There is no momentum in sitting on the fence.

"Could you build your current business up, hire a salesperson then sell it?" I asked. "It would give you the freedom you want."

"It doesn't interest me to build and sell it. I still want to have a business. I like being a business owner and the people I meet. I enjoy the business conventions in great travel locations, and I don't want to give it up."

Every decision—for or against—can move you forward. Knowing what you don't want—like complete retirement—can help you clarify what you do want.

Greg's "Why" suddenly had more clarity.

"What do you really want?"

He told me he was looking into purchasing an existing brick and mortar business complete with salespeople. Yes, an early retirement seemed appealing, but without some continuing business income, he couldn't afford to keep his current lifestyle.

He talked about profits, the number of hours per week he wanted to work, and hiring a manager for day-to-day operations. "But why? What will this dream give you?"

"I'm 57," he said. "I want time to enjoy more of life while I'm still young enough."

Simon Sinek had it right: Start with Why. Now we knew what Greg really wanted—business ownership, travel, association with other business owners, and limited working hours, we could plot out his next steps.

What do you really want from your business? Why this dream?

For your dream to matter to you, it needs to offer you something, something more personal than "making a difference" or "changing the world." When your dream comes to fruition, what is your expectation? What will it give you?

For example, your dream may be a six-figure business working only 30 hours per week. The purpose behind your dream may be to spend more time with your family. To travel. To free you up to do mission work for your church. To demonstrate to your children success is possible. To provide top care for your aging parents. To live the life you've always dreamed.

Your purpose reflects your personal core values.

If it weren't for your Purpose, the dream might not matter so much. Your purpose keeps you going when the path to your dream looks like Mission Impossible. It can also be a guiding light when making practical decisions about your business: will this decision help fulfill your purpose?

Your Purpose is not something you typically share with your client (although you might).

Greg answered this question. Now he consults with other online entrepreneurs, travels, and speaks at business retreats and conferences while working 15-20 hours per week and nets more than he did with his online parts business. He also feels more fulfilled knowing he is making a difference to these small business owners.

Take some time now and journal the Purpose behind your dream, your Why.

In Summary

The four steps to define/refine your dream—to be certain of what you want— are:

1. How have you defined your dream so far?
2. Do you still want the same dream?
   If not, then What?
3. Is it yours?
4. Why do you want it?

By the way, "waiting for the morning" was a long time ago for me. Life is so much more fun now that I have my What and Why.

Chapter 4

Having Fun?

Business Is No Fun Anymore

Have you ever thought to yourself, this is just not fun anymore? Whether your business, career, life, or relationship, sometimes the thought pops out unexpectedly: it's just no fun anymore!

Google describes fun as enjoyment, amusement, or lighthearted pleasure and adds in synonyms like enjoyment, entertainment, and pleasure. Wikipedia says fun is "an enjoyable distraction, diverting the mind and body from any serious task or contributing an extra dimension to it."

It's the "contributing an extra dimension" to serious tasks I'm talking about here. Fun doesn't just take place during play and recreation. You can bring that "extra dimension" into any part of your business day, whether meeting with your team or producing your next product.

But things can seem so serious. The thought, "This is no fun anymore!" can sneak up on you, sometimes slowly until one day, like quicksand, you find yourself sucked into a feeling of discontent about your business, your life. Struggle against this feeling and it sucks you in faster until you're pulled under, suffocated by the un-funness of it all.

Nothing is safe from the "no fun" monster. It can attack not only your income-creating business, but also the business of your life: relationships, parenting, the car you drive, even your vacation!

My Toughest Lesson: Fun

Fun. This may have been the toughest of my lessons. My Dutch father and a puritanical mother raised me to have a strong work ethic. Fun was not approved unless the work was done, and the work was never done.

This work ethic served me well in my business, but it was especially hard on relationships. I will always regret the time I missed playing with my son as he grew up. I always hated it when someone asked me, "What do you do for fun?" I didn't do anything for fun. I didn't have a clue how to answer their question. So I began exploring: what was fun for me? I enjoyed reading (caught in snatches here and there) and jigsaw puzzles (a rare occurrence, usually late in the evening and stretched out over a few weeks).

The turning point came when my health took a hit with adrenal burnout. I could barely make it through the day. Something had to give. With the help of friends and coaches, I started adding fun to my life. The toughest part was figuring out what was fun for me. I was out of touch with the concept of fun. I started slowly, and won't bore you with the entire journey, but here are a few things I learned.

Fun Is Subjective

While I enjoy Sudoku (a numbers puzzle) and reading, other people would rather do anything else! A good friend of mine loves climbing trees and buys an annual membership to a local adventure course where she climbs, zip-lines, and swings from ropes. Not my cup of tea. Some people love to be in the water, diving or swimming. I love to be on or near the water, boating or beaching. Fun is personal.

The Fun of Doing

As a break from all the work I did, I started a Meetup group. Its sole purpose was to host fun-for-me outings. If you haven't heard of Meetup.com, it's an online service where people sponsor or join local activities of their choosing, from business to biking, from networking to knitting. You can be part of a community—based on activities you enjoy—within any number of miles of your zip code.

If you are a Meetup host, your role is to show up to your events. Hosting forced me out of the house. I did things I'd been putting off: bridge walks, outings to the Big Cat Habitat, music festivals, dancing, sunset boat cruises, a visit to the Sarasota Whimsical Museum, and even a day trip to a Blueberry Festival. I made some great new friends through the Meetup.

Fun During a Business Day

Next, I started adding small bits of fun into my business day in the form of simple, refreshing ten-minute breaks. If I need to clear my mind, a walk around the block for some fresh air does the trick. When my energy runs low, I put on an upbeat tune and dance around the office. Or maybe I relax and change my head space as I sit on the porch for ten minutes with a good book. It's become a habit. This boosts my productivity and I feel less stressed at the end of the day.

These breaks, these bits of fun, has given me a bonus I hadn't expected: I have the energy for even more fun during the evening.

Crenshaw's book, *The Power of Fun*[2] (Berrett-Koehler Publishers; ©2017), is all about how scheduling several fun breaks during the day actually increases productivity. Studies show people who take time out for fun are healthier and happier. Corporations pay him money to make fun happen!

In his book *Rest: Why You Get More Done When You Work Less* (Basic Books; ©2016), Alex Soojung-Kim Pang discusses an observation shared by top scientists: "time relaxing or engaging in hobbies could be

---

[2] Go to www.askShauna.com/BONUS for links and resources and more.

valuable, while low achievers had no hobbies or found them irrelevant."

Act like a top-performer: dedicate time for fun and play.

Exercise: How to Expand the Fun Factor

Life and business can—and should!—be fun. There are three steps to expand the fun factor in your business and your life:

1. Know what you want.
2. Create a vision to inspire you.
3. Enjoy the journey.

Let's take a deeper look.

1. Know what you want.

What makes you happy? What do you enjoy? What is fun for you?

You can do this exercise in a 30-60 minute brainstorming session, or keep a notepad (smartphone notepads and Evernote are always with you!) to create a list over the course of a week during coffee breaks, while you are on hold, or during your walk or workout.

Go crazy! Take time to dream. Make it big. Don't miss the little things. This is about desire, not immediate possibilities. Here's an idea-generating list of Career-Related Things from American Writers to get you started.

- Reach a fabled level of success to make you untouchable
- Create a positive work/life balance
- Feel as capable as others think you are
- Be more productive with each minute of the day
- Be recognized as talented or even brilliant
- Pursue your calling while supporting your family financially
- Make enough money to care for aging parents

Now it's your turn. Take a moment and write down what you truly want from your business.

Creating a
vision board
is probably
one of the
most valuable
visualization
tools available to you.

Jack Canfield

2. Create a vision to inspire you.

A Huffington Post writer conducted a survey of 700 people. She asked: "If you could say in one word what you want more of in life, what would that be?"

The number one answer: Happiness.

Then she asked them: "What is the biggest challenge in the way of having Happiness?"

Their answer: "Not knowing what I want to do."

In step one, you identified what you want. Now you expand your ideas into a three-dimensional vision to help you Expand the Fun Factor both intellectually and visually.

The Intellectual Method: Goal Setting

A small but highly successful portion of the population sets written goals. Studies show those who review their goals frequently are even more successful.

There are a lot of methods (as you can see if you Google "goal-setting tips"). The simplest method is one a coach had me do years ago. She told me to write out 100 goals—business or personal, near-term or far future; it didn't matter. I created the list over the course of a week. As I wrote down my goals, it made the possibility of having them more real and put a big smile on my face.

When the list was complete, I tucked it away somewhere. When I found it a couple of years later, I was amazed how many things I hadn't given any attention which I could now cross off. I still have things I haven't done (like a trip to Tahiti), but life isn't over yet!

The Visual Method: Make a Vision Board

If you aren't much into lists and formal processes, try this option to help create a vision to inspire you. This one can be downright fun!

Are you familiar with vision boards? Wikipedia defines a vision board as a collage of images, pictures, and affirmations of your dreams. It's a picture of things to make you happy. Think of it as a visual version of goal-setting.

Designer Kelly Hoppen says, "A vision board is about what you want and how you'll achieve it. If you think of your brain as a messy room, a vision board is like tidying it up."

Every year during my birthday month I hold a vision board party. Besides the food, drink, and camaraderie, here's how it goes:

Step 1: Grab a stack of old magazines and cut out pictures of things representing what you want to be, do, or have.

Step 2: Have fun arranging the pictures on the board any which way you want, then paste them onto paper or poster-board. (I use a sheet from a 12"x18" sketch pad.)

Step 3: Post it where you will see it often. It will work on your conscious and subconscious to make your dreams happen. (The documentary "The Secret," available on Netflix, helps explain how this works.)

For more details on how to create your vision board, check out these two resources[3]:

- How to create a vision board (businessinsider.com)

- The Reason Vision Boards Work and How to Make One (huffingtonpost.com)

---

[3] Go to www.askShauna.com/BONUS for links and resources and more.

According to Forbes magazine, "Psychologists from the University of California who study happiness found that genetics and life circumstances only account for about 50% of a person's happiness. The rest is up to you."

This is one of my
personal visions boards.

If you are genuinely on the path to what you want, you may experience ups, downs, and bumps in the road—even while holding your vision. But underneath it all, you will feel a sense of joy, peace, and purpose.

3. Enjoy the journey.

Life doesn't always go as planned. (That's why we call it an adventure!) So what to do when plans go awry? Enjoy the journey.

You can try to skip this step, but it will only make you grouchy. The journey provides information and growth to prepare you for arrival at your destination. Appreciate the journey: you are becoming someone more than you used to be.

Do what you need to make your journey more enjoyable. It might mean taking more breaks. Find support (a session with your coach, a cozy chat with a girlfriend, a reach-out to a supportive private Facebook group).

Revel in the adventure. Value all progress. Enjoy the little things along the way.

The thrill of reaching the destination doesn't last all that long. Relish the thrill of anticipation by keeping your eyes on the vision that inspires each step. Play the game of time and enjoy the journey that shows up.

Business can be fun! Let's recap those steps:

- Know What You Want
- Create a Vision To Inspire You
- Enjoy the journey

Chapter 5

Overcome Overwhelm

Overwhelm Can Kill

Overwhelm kills. Well, think about it. Doesn't overwhelm cause stress? And isn't stress a known killer? Stress undermines our sanity, our sleep, and ultimately our health.

- Does overwhelm drive you crazy?
- Are you so buried in your work you haven't seen your family in three days?
- Is your business taking over your life?

Being overwhelmed can kill your passion—both in business and in relationships.

I think most of us became business owners because we have something to share. We want the flexible lifestyle of not reporting to someone else. We have something we're passionate about and are paid to do what we love.

But if your business takes too much out of you, you become overwhelmed. Sometimes all it takes is thinking about all there is to do! Either way, you end up stressed, lose your passion, and the business you once loved can become a grind.

Overwhelm paralyzes possibility. It holds you back from the lifestyle and income waiting for you. It suffocates your soul. It kills. It kills you, your business, and your success.

Who wants to live this way? It's time to break free.

Three Steps Out Of Overwhelm

In the book, *How To Be Rich And Happy*, (Aspen Light Publishing; © 2009), the authors Strelecky and Brownson talk about doing less and getting more done. Rich and happy people do what they love and create incredible income. Because they love the work they do, they produce quality results in less time.

Which brings us to our first overwhelm buster:

1. Cut back on tasks you don't like to focus on the work you love.

It's not only three-year-olds who can say "I don't wanna." We all have preferences and aversions. There are some things I, personally, do not want to do but sometimes must, like reconciling my bank statements because my assistant is on vacation.

"Cut back on tasks I don't like?" you ask. "But what I don't like is critical to keeping me in business. If I cut back in those, I could lose everything."

Maybe, maybe not. Let's go with "maybe." If it is a critical task and you don't love it, look at hiring or outsourcing. Yes, yes. It can cost money to hire help. But not always! There are alternatives. We'll talk about this in a minute.

It might also mean restructuring your business model. A friend of mine had a successful multi-six-figure business, but she wasn't happy. She had been running the same program, marketed the same way, for nearly six years. There were always new clients because of the results she provided, but she did more public speaking and more workshops than she was personally comfortable with (she's a bit of an introvert).

Her efforts, as uncomfortable as they were, produced a good income, so she was reluctant to change anything. Fortunately, she listened to the coaching and transformed her business model into one in sync with whom she is at her core. She now works less and makes even more.

Aside from restructuring your business model (which we delve into in the *Time to Thrive* program), here are three steps to help you eliminate or minimize tasks you'd rather escape.

First, identify tasks you don't like!

Yes, you heard me correctly. Identify what you spend time on—including the things you don't enjoy. Look at how much time you're spending there. When I added up the amount of time spent on email, I was horrified.

The good news is—once you see it, you can do something about it. Identifying and quantifying is the first step. (See Chapter 6 for tips on how to minimize your time on email, even without unsubscribing.)

Second, group similar tasks.

Grouping tasks to complete is another way to minimize how long they will take. I learned this trick years ago, and it really works! For example, if you have five phone calls to make today, and you do one every hour or so, it will take longer collectively to make those five calls than if you sat and made them all back to back.

There is also a best time of day for specific activities. Errands, for me, are best done mid-afternoon. By then I've been at my desk long enough. My mind wants to take a break. My body needs to move. Email, unless I'm watching for something in particular, I relegate to once a day, typically late afternoon or evening.

Ask yourself, which groups can you complete once a week (or less) instead of once a day?

I only open snail-mail once a week, except for books and supplies I order online. My assistant brings in the mail and puts it in the appointed holding place. Once a week she slices open and pulls content out of the envelopes.

She files the standard credit card and bank statements, and leaves me two piles (grouping, again). One might be junk, for me to check it before I toss it; the other pile needs my action (things like unpaid invoices and forms she needs the information to fill and return).

Here are some other ideas for weekly or less frequent activities:

- Do your bookkeeping once a week, if you do your own, rather than squeezing it in between other tasks all week long.
- Develop and schedule your social media posts once a week.
- If you create videos, you can designate one day every couple of weeks and create several all at once, then queue them to publish when you want.

Grouping tasks is one of the best ways to save time.

Third, hire or outsource.

Back to the list of things you don't want to do. Who can do it for you? Here are a few ways to find help with minimal cost.

Intern: Depending on what you need help with, you may want to hire a college intern. One of my clients did this for her acupuncture practice; she wanted to document the office procedures. Sherri works only for a few hours once a week, but processes are being documented, which means less time training her next office admin, and it's helping identify holes in her procedures. Interns are typically inexpensive; they need college credit and real-life experience.

Outsource: Can you outsource these tasks? Whether it's something simple (set up an email series to send to your list, design a logo or infographic, or make phone calls) or something complex (design an app, manage your video or YouTube marketing), there is someone who can do it for you.

Virtual Assistant: For ongoing office admin (tasks to work on remotely, like research, updating your Facebook business page, or posting articles or blogs), a Virtual Assistant (often abbreviated to VA) is an excellent choice. You can avoid payroll issues and the logistics of providing an extra office space or supplies. According to Entrepreneur magazine[4], a Virtual Assistant is the fastest ticket to growth for entrepreneurs.

Freelancers: There are several VA websites, and you can find VAs and other freelancers in online resources like Fiverr.com (yes, Fiverr with two r's), Freelancer.com, and Upwork.com are two of the most

---

[4] Go to www.askShauna.com/BONUS for links and resources and more.

If you ask
more of yourself
than time allows,
you get out of
balance.

Abraham-Hicks

popular. (Fiverr is best for quick, one-shot, clearly defined assignments.) These sites provide various skill sets from freelancers who work from all over the world, novice to expert, along with an easy way to pay safely (often with-holding payment to the freelancer until you've approved the final result).

If you work is time-based (e.g., by the hour), they often have ways to monitor the hours billed so you can confirm they spent time on your project and not surfing the internet or taking care of another client.

And that, dear friends, is how you cut back on tasks you don't like to leave you free to focus on the work you love:

- Identify tasks you don't like.
- Group similar tasks.
- Hire or outsource.

2. Set boundaries against burnout.

The second step to leaving overwhelm behind is to set boundaries. Setting boundaries mean saying yes to what works, and no to everything else. Symptoms of a lack of boundaries include:

- You try to please everyone
- You try to help everyone
- You try to do everything
- You try to know everything
- You try to be everything

A colleague of mine, Ken McArthur, identified those in his column "How to Do More, Working With Less." It's a good reminder for us *"I have to do everything myself"* small businesses owners.

I dedicate a full training module on how to set and hold your boundaries in *Time to Thrive*. It's that important.

3. Hire coaches and mentors.

Just like a professional baseball player may have a batting coach as well as a strength and conditioning coach, financial coach, nutrition coach, so many successful small business owners have more than one coach, each specializing in a different area.

You might have a business strategist, a financial coach, a mindset coach, and a marketing coach. If you struggle with cash flow, sometimes you can make a trade of your services for theirs. Find ways to make it work for you. Even a free strategy session from the right person can move you forward. Those sessions also help you interview potential coaches to see who resonates.

None of us can be successful in a vacuum. No matter how good you are at what you do, sometimes you are too close to the trees to see the forest. We need mentors and coaches for the perspective, suggestions, guidance, and expertise they bring. They can help you stay focused, on track. A coach can save you time, heartache, and thousands of dollars.

Identify the expertise you most need and find a way to hire them.

To Summarize the Three Step Solution

1. Cut back on tasks you don't like to focus on the work you love.
2. Set boundaries against burnout.
3. Hire coaches and mentors.

I refer to these steps myself whenever I am in overwhelm. Yes, overwhelm still happens, but using these steps, it disappears quickly!

Chapter 6

Twenty-four Hours a Day

My Journey With Time

In the past few years I've learned so much about caring for my time. Not long ago, I was convinced there was never time for fun and very little time for me. To "prove" it, I worked all the time—doing everything from the day job, a business venture, or the chores of maintaining a home, etc.

Then I hit burnout. I was so tired I could barely make it from the bed to kitchen to the couch. My doctor said, "Rest."

I needed support to rebuild my adrenals (those little glands stimulated during fight-or-flight). It seems my life had been one long fight-or-flight to keep a decent income as a single mom and sole provider.

Working with a health practitioner helped me regain my energy. (Adrenal recovery takes a few years when it became as bad as mine.) I started working with a business coach who inspired insights that gave me my life back, providing more fun and more time for me.

I understood time in a way I never had before. After learning the methods, magic, and mindset on the road to mastering time, I wanted to share these lessons to make it easier for others who struggle with the same issues, so I began this book.

But Life laughed at me and turned the tables upside down—again. I was working full-time, writing a book, and starting a new relationship. There was no time left for Shauna. I was writing about time but had no time and instead was risking adrenal burnout, round two.

Life works in mysterious ways. Coming up against the very thing I wanted to help others with meant I had to go deeper. So I did.

Here is what I learned about the *Five Truths of Time* as I peeled back the next layers.

The First Truth of Time

> Each day gives you 24 hours.
> It's yours to spend
> however you choose.

This is great news! Time is a never-ending supply, but you can't have it all at one time. That would be crazy-making. "The only reason for time is so everything doesn't happen at once." (Albert Einstein)

If we had double the time (two chunks of time, both at the same time) we would waste one of the two chunks. Sort of like fine dining: you can only eat one meal at a time. We feel bloated and uncomfortable if we try to stuff too much food in at once.

Divine wisdom ("God," by whatever name you use) dispenses time in 24-hour increments to align with our linear use of time. The fresh block of 24 hours you receive each day might seem to be not enough, but it helps level the playing field. No one receives any more than you. If they seem to have more time, they are merely spending it differently.

You have the power to choose how you spend your time.

I often hear my clients singing a tune with lyrics like this: "There is more work than I can do." "I have a lot of obligations." "My family needs me." "My client needs me now."

I know this song intimately. Before I learned the *Truths of Time*, I would often say to my friends, "I need 36 hours a day... more would be better." I worked hard and pushed the edges of my day, focused on work and obligations. On top of my work, there were bills to pay, dinners to prepare, kitchens to clean, clothes and linens to launder. As a single mom, the list was never-ending.

Not all at Once!

Making sure everything doesn't happen at once is a practical decision! We live in a physical world; some things are logistically impossible. Can you imagine wanting to stretch, eat an ice cream cone, and smell a rose all in the same instant of time?

- When you stretch your arms, it would move the cone away from your face; you would need a giraffe's neck and the agility of a contortionist to lick the cone.

- If you lick the cone and swallow while at the same time deeply breathing in the scent of the rose, the wrong stuff would go down your windpipe and leave you in a fit of coughing.

- You could stretch and smell a rose at the same time, but how could you thoroughly enjoy the stretch if you are distracted by the focus on breathing in the scent of the rose? Unless someone is holding the rose to your nose while you close your eyes and savor the stretch, you would lose out on the full luxury of each experience.

But you want to do so many different things, right? I do too. Regrettably, we can't do all of them this very minute. This is where priorities come into play.

"Right Now!" Priorities

There are Life priorities and there are "right this minute" priorities. The best "right this minute" priorities respect your values and your Life priorities.

- Time does not care who you are or what you have or haven't done up to this point in your life. It doesn't care what your plans are for the

Each day
you are given
24 hours.
It's yours to **spend**
however you choose.

1st Truth of Time

future. It doesn't care if you use it wisely, or if you squander it. It only pays attention to "right now"—the present moment.

During my workaholic lifestyle, I operated from a very narrow focus. I gave my "right this minute" priorities over to an old work ethic my dad gave me: "You can't have fun while there's work to be done." Trying to live up to this discipline eventually led me to adrenal burnout. My body said "Stop! I can't do this anymore." It took adrenal burnout for me to claim "health" as one of my core values. I had been taking it for granted!

Once my values were clear, things began to shift. It took more than a year to recover enough of my energy to pursue my business dream once again.

Now, even when I have a deadline, I will take "right now" time for a break. It can be as quick as a two-minute stretch or a fresh cup of tea; or it can be a longer relaxing/energizing evening out with friends eating, dancing, or listening to a band play.

A corollary to the *First Truth of Time* is:

> Only I have the final say on
> how I spend my 24 hours.

Quick Tips to spend your 24 hours more wisely.

The first and fastest way to get back time is to streamline low-payback activities... like email.

Email consumed way too much of my time, so I started here. With a couple of simple tools and practices, I brought my email under control. I used spend too much time trying to set up filters to make sure I always saw the essential emails first.

Everything changed when I started using these tools (they work with several email providers from Gmail to Outlook).

Easy Email Streamlining Tools

If you need to keep your eye on your email Inbox throughout the day, use these tools to keep less important emails out of sight to look at later.

Unroll.me

With unroll.me, emails you have subscribed to automatically move into a separate folder, keeping everything you want to be aware in an easy-access spot. They capture a snapshot of the first part of each email into a single daily digest called the Rollup. This digest appears in your Inbox every day at the time you choose. One email. All your subscriptions. Done.

This product, amazingly, is free. There are ads in the rollup email which, to me, are non-intrusive. I can quickly scan or ignore them along with all the emails rolled up for the day.

SaneBox

SaneBox works anywhere you check your email, on your desktop or mobile, and email providers from Gmail to Outlook. They offer a generous free trial, and it's inexpensive; it more than pays for itself in time saved. You can send mail to Later, Snooze, Tomorrow, and more. SaneBox lets you take back control. I love it!

Email is only one area where you can save time by streamlining low-payback activities. For more timesaving tools, download my free e-book—Ten Top Timesavers—and more at askShauna.com/BONUS.

The Practice: Time-Blocking

Here is a time-blocking tactic—a powerful time saver! (I talk more about time-blocking in the *Fourth Truth of Time*.) Stop the email interruptions! There are very few instances, unless your business runs on email, where people need an immediate reply. As anyone who receives a personal email from me could tell you, below my signature lines there is an additional line stating:

> As a proponent of time blocking,
> I check email 1-2x/day.

When someone sends something they need me to check sooner than "at my convenience," they text: "Check your email."

Details That Save You

When you have more to do than you can accomplish in a day, use this strategy to make the most of your precious 24 hours: identify the details of your day and plan your approach.

Now you may think, "I don't have time for planning; I need to get something done NOW." But remember the story of the woodsman who said, "Give me five minutes to chop down a tree, and I will spend the first two-and-a-half minutes sharpening the axe." This little exercise is worth the time.

1. Make a list of everything you need to accomplish.
2. Include major project milestones you must meet.
3. Include filing, phone calls, lunch, laundry, errands, and planned interruptions like the kids coming home from school. All of these take time. Plan on it!
4. Next, put a time estimate next to each. It's not rocket science. Give it your best guesstimate. For example, "phone the plumber" might take 10 minutes. However, if you forgot the name of the guy you used last and you go look for it or call a friend to see who they recommend, allow more time.
5. Tally up the time.

Last time I did this the day I'd mapped out totaled 18 hours. The following steps are what pared it down from crazy-making to a day where I accomplished a lot and felt relaxed in the process. This stuff really works!

6. Glance at your list and cross of whatever can wait until tomorrow.//
7. Of what's left, pick the top item.
8. Do only one thing. Don't do anything else until this one is complete.
9. Repeat steps 7 and 8 until done — or time for a break!.

Go ahead, sharpen your axe. Run through the exercise on the days there is way too much to get done and see for yourself how it can trim time spent and help you focus on what's most important.

My highest vision for my life includes fun, health, and relaxation. Amazingly, I'm getting more done now than when I was trying to push upstream constantly.

Remember the First Truth of Time

Each day gives you24 hours.
It's yours to spend however you choose.

Chapter 7

Time Is For Sale

The Second Truth of Time:
Time is for sale; you can buy more.

Time is for sale, and there is a price. You have to give up doing everything yourself.

"No one else can do it as well as I can."

Perhaps. Or perhaps they can do it better or faster. Maybe perfection is one of your obstacles. Inc. Magazine says, "Perfection is the enemy of success. Don't let it be." Forbes identifies the seeking of perfection as one of the greatest errors in business.

Smallbiztrends.com says, "Always trying to be perfect eliminates your inclination to take risks and innovate. You need to be creative to thrive in business." They advise instead you strive for consistency.

Consistency is easier when you have the support and the people, to ensure it.

"But it's easier to do it myself!" you argue.

Yes, maybe the first time, and even the second or third time. If the task is something you do once a week, and it takes an hour each time, you have just spent 50 hours, which is more than the standard USA 40-hour workweek.

Wouldn't you rather savor an extra week on vacation with your family, invest the time in a couple of three-day business-growing retreats, or use it to work on the parts of your business you most enjoy? Find three tasks to offload, and you have 150 hours back—nearly four workweeks.

Still worried about the hassle of teaching someone something you know how to do? Try these steps to take the drudgery out of repetitive tasks.

5 Easy Steps To Systematize Repetitive Processes

Did you ever hire someone to do a task… or worse, NOT hire the help you needed because you didn't have time to train them? Systematizing a repetitive process takes a bit of extra work up front, but it pays when you can hand something off having confidence they will do it to your specifications, leaving YOU free to leverage your genius.

To simultaneously train your new hire and create a written process for whomever may do the task when they move on, follow these steps.

First: identify a task to systematize.

Select one of your recurring tasks. What could you turn into a written procedure? Pick an irritating task, something that causes you grief or costs you too much time. Let's remove it first.

Second: Log. Every. Step.

Next time you—or your assistant—does this task… Log. Every. Step.

You're probably thinking, "Who has time for THAT!" Sounds a bit overwhelming or tedious, doesn't it? It's not... when you delegate it to the person you hired. You would train them anyway. Have them create detailed notes each step of the way.

1. The process could be as simple as a list of steps, in sequence. A checklist.

2. If it's a computer task, use a good screen capture software to create visuals to go with the checklist. Remember, a picture is worth a thousand words. (I like SnagIt because you can easily annotate it with arrows, circles, callout notes... all kinds of good stuff.)

Afterwards your trainee types up their notes and puts them into a simple step-by-step list. This is the first draft. It doesn't have to be perfect at this point. Set the rough draft aside. Nothing else to do until it's time to repeat the task.

Third: Validate the documented steps, real-time.

The next time you need to do the task, pull out the first draft. Ask whoever will follow the steps (even if they are the person who documented the procedures) to follow each step listed as if they never worked on it before.

1. If they are about to do a step and it's not on the list, have them stop and add it.
2. If it is difficult to understand a step, have them update the instructions.

With my new-hire going through a task only the second time, I usually am there with them as part of the training process to point out what to add or clarify.

Again, don't worry about perfection. We aren't done yet. This is merely an updated first draft.

Fourth: Audit with fresh eyes.

The <u>next</u> time you need to do the task, either give it to someone who hasn't tried it before (fresh eyes, so to speak) or have your new-hire go through it without you hovering. Ask them to follow the checklist and to stop and ask questions any time a step isn't entirely clear.

This will help you identify holes in the process. Then update the document to clarify steps and add explanations useful to a "new" person.

Time is **for sale**.
You can buy more.

2nd Truth of Time

Fifth: File it in your procedures manual.

Put the final document in your new Company Procedures Manual (sometimes called an Operations Manual). This is the place where you keep all of your procedures (usually digital; I call my folder "Procedures").

You're Hired!

Rose used to struggle with time. (Remember her from Chapter One?) There was never enough. She came to me because she wanted to increase her revenues.

The first assignment I gave her was to hire a full-time office assistant—someone to answer phones, schedule client appointments, open, shelve, and ring up sales for the boxes of incoming product each week.

"I don't need someone full-time," Rose argued at first, but after we reviewed her typical work week—staying late, working through lunch, coming in on weekends to catch up—she reluctantly agreed to hire someone on a 30-day trial.

We used my hiring process to narrow the list of applicants quickly. Within two weeks after her new assistant started, Rose said, "I don't know how I ever made it without her!"

Rose finally had room to breathe, was sleeping better, and her mind was clear and able to make better decisions. We outlined simple marketing and pricing strategies to triple her revenues quickly.

Hiring someone is one way to make or take time back for yourself. For Rose, it started with the decision to stop working nights and weekends and hire some help.

The Price and Benefits

The price

Time is for sale, and there is a price. Besides the cost of the new employee or contractor and your up-front investment of time to find, hire, and sometimes train them, there are some things you may need to give up. Things like perfection, control of the minutia, the chaos of "winging it."

The benefits

Time is for sale, and there are benefits:

- Accomplish a task or project in hours instead of the days it might take you to accomplish the same thing.
- Create greater consistency for your clients.
- Tackle projects you don't have the skill set for (like redoing the website or planning an event to boost your business).
- Step back from the day-to-day tasks.
- Accomplish more (after all, there is more than one of you now).

What would it feel like to have all those benefits along with more time and less stress? Give yourself the gift of support. It's more fun and less lonely.

Remember the Second Truth of Time

Time is for sale; you can buy more.

Chapter 8

Personal Time

No Respect

"How could she?" I felt completely disrespected.

I was still working my day job and spending evenings and weekends preparing my new business for launch. My boss asked for an extra report which took me another 20 hours over a period of two weeks—on top of my other work! Most of it, of course, accomplished during unpaid overtime. I submitted it on time, and she said, "Oh, we don't need that after all."

"How could she!"

It wasn't just my boss disrespecting my efforts. Friends weren't showing up when they said they would. Colleagues regularly arrived late to my meetings. People were cutting me off on the road. I felt disrespected all over the place. What was going on here?

The Universe listens when I ask questions, always ready with an answer in one form or another. (Years ago I cultivated the habit of listening to the whisper of a higher power. Now I receive answers, even when I ask a rhetorical question!) This time the answer came in the form of a quote by author Katherine Woodward Thomas:

"If you find others treat you with disrespect, instead of complaining and making them wrong, ask yourself in what ways you are disrespecting yourself."

So I looked at my own behavior.

- I had been disrespecting my health by pushing myself, working when I needed more rest.

- I had been disrespecting time for myself: I couldn't remember the last time I took a full day off (not even a Sunday!).

- I had been disrespecting my home. The kitchen was a mess. My cluttered home office barely left room to work, and the dirty clothes hamper was spilling over.

How could I expect others to respect me when I wouldn't even respect myself? I made more demands on myself than I could handle, then beat myself up for what I couldn't do.

Have you ever had clients making more demands on you than you feel you can deal with? Have you made more demands on yourself than you would anyone else? Did you start the business to see how hard you can work? Me neither, but all I did was work hard until I discovered the *Third Truth of Time*.

The Third Truth of Time

Personal time: You can only have as much as you take.

Time is a fickle beast, but she responds well to outright demands. When you insist there isn't enough time, she will cooperate and make herself scarce. When you reach the end of your rope and declare, "Enough! I'm taking some time for Me!" only then will Time respond and say, "You can have as much personal time as you take."

"But there is too much to do," you say. Of course, there is. Don't worry. It will be there when you come

You can only
have as much
personal time
as you take.

3rd Truth of Time

back from the time you take. Does it frighten you that "it"—whatever is on those long lists of yours—will still be there?

There is a secret to dealing with those lists. We cover this topic in detail in *Time to Thrive*, but here is a quick trick to practice immediately:

Learn to say No

It's amazing how, when you get knocked on your ass (which is what adrenal burnout feels like), you gain a new perspective. I realized during the low of my burnout how much time I gave away—especially to clients. I was proud of over delivering. I hadn't realized over delivering, in my case, too often meant I was working for little to no pay.

"Just a quick question," former or would-be clients would say. Their question was quick, but it evoked a dozen questions I needed to ask them to clarify their situation. Often my answer turned into a strategy session where I gave them a plan of action to increase their sales, improve their marketing, or help them deal with a difficult client.

Even for paying clients, I gave above and beyond what they had originally hired me to do. But my health was at risk. I started to

say "No." I wouldn't be able to serve anyone if I didn't take care of me first.

I said "No" to networking events that drained my energy and never brought new business. At my lowest point, I was even saying no to most lunch and dinner invitations with friends. I didn't have the energy.

Don't let depleted energy or a health scare be your wake-up call. Learn to say "No." Only you have the final say on how you spend your time.

One of the most effective ways to take back time is to say "No."

Take care of your most important asset: You! Of the time given to you each day, be like a tiger with her cubs. Plan and guard your personal hours, the time you need for sleep, self-care, and replenishment. Let no one take it away.

Your life depends on it.

Remember the Third Truth of Time:

> Personal time: You can only have as much as you take.

Chapter 9

Time Hides

The Fourth Truth of Time

Have you ever come to the end of your day and say, "What happened?" You were well-intentioned when you began. There were things you needed to do. You may have done some of them. But overall, the day wasted away in a little bit of this, a little of that.

The Fourth Truth of Time:

> Time hides in the craziest places. Reclaim your time.

Let's explore where time can hide.

The Internet

One of the rabbit holes my time likes to disappear into is the internet—both email and web browsing. It's not just cat videos that grab people's time and attention. I love information about all things business and marketing, but even that can be a distraction from what I need to do.

For example, take the daily emails I receive from Inc.com. They are one of my favorite attention-grabbers. I use Unroll.me (the free tool I mentioned earlier) to remove the temptation to view these information-packed emails during the day, but when I review the daily roll-up, I will see snapshots of articles from INC.com. I try to ignore them, but find myself clicking through to some.

As you can imagine, one thing leads to another and I am soon way down the rabbit hole of distractions, reading far and wide on various topics. As much fun as it can be, I want my time back.

I remembered something I had once read about a software which limits how long you spend on the internet, or on a list of selected time-consuming websites. Of course, I researched it.

Cleverly (or so I thought) I decided to time how long this research took. (Being a details nerd can be so painful at times!) I set my iPhone stopwatch and started my search. When I came up for air 45 minutes later, I had researched prices on a couple of things I needed for the house, placed three Amazon orders, emailed my sister and replied to a text.

But no, I still hadn't found the "Don't let me lose myself on the internet!" web blocker, but I did find something better... once I resumed my original research.

RescueTime tracks where you spend your computer time and comes with the free version. I opted for the paid version (only $9/month at the time of this publication) to gain the ability to block distracting websites.

Be sure to grab a complimentary copy of my e-book, *Ten Top Timesavers*[5]. The video accelerator plugin is one of my favorites; it saves me hours every week. (I listen to motivational or business YouTube channels while I dress each morning.)

---

[5] Available at www.AskShauna.com/Bonus

Time hides
in the
craziest
places.
Reclaim
your time.

4th Truth of Time

Interrupted vs. In The Groove

Internet browsing is only one place time hides. Interruptions is another.

Based on a study at the University of California, Irvine, it takes an average of 23 minutes and 15 seconds to return to a task after being interrupted. Yes, it takes time to get back in the groove. Even if the interruptions are only once a day (and we know it's typically more!), you lose nearly 100 hours or two-and-a-half weeks per year.

What could you do with an extra two-and-a-half weeks? And how on earth do you eliminate distractions? Identifying them is the first step. When it comes to outside forces—phone calls, texts, people dropping by—learning to set boundaries is key. (Remember what we said about boundaries in the last chapter.)

Chores: Who does them?

Another place time hides is in those pesky everyday chores—things like laundry, cleaning, paying the bills, watering the plants, and feeding the dog. These chores can subtly (or not-so-subtly) eat away at your time. If you have a work-from-home business—especially then!—the chores of life can destroy a productive workday. Work-from-home or not, business chores can do the same thing.

In the office, a good assistant can make all the difference. At home, simply having a housecleaning service—even if it's only once a month—gives you valuable time back.

Time Blocking

One of the tricks to productivity (another name for spending time wisely) is time blocking. What is time blocking? It is the opposite of scattered action.

Time blocking is the act of grouping similar tasks and blocking a time to handle the group. (We touched on grouping in Chapter 5.) Let me give you an example of how time blocking works. On one of my recent Plan-the-Day lists (which I always write out when it looks like there is more to do than I can do in one day), I boiled all my tasks into these categories:

- At my computer: offline ("airplane mode" tasks like updating documents)
- At my computer (projects): online research, reviewing the updates to my website
- At my computer (admin): Emails, social media, placing orders, buying a new domain
- Connecting: Phone calls, scheduled appointments (some via Zoom), follow-ups, proactive reach-out
- Accounting (some online and some offline tasks)
- Errands and chores

Mixing up a block of "at the computer" tasks with activities away from it helps keep you fresh. Time blocking makes your time efficient instead of chaotic.

Examine each area of your business, your life. Where can you reclaim time?

Remember the Fourth Truth of Time:

Time hides in the craziest places. Reclaim your time.

In *Time to Thrive*, we drill deeper into these and other areas to uncover the activities hiding time. Meanwhile, reclaim some of your time now by implementing a few of these ideas. Choose one or two right now to put into action.

Chapter 10

Time is Like a Lover

The Fifth Truth of Time

Have you ever been so up against time that, try as you might, nothing seems to get done?

> Time is like a lover. It responds to
> the attention you give it.

Like a lover, Time has its idiosyncrasies. It responds to the way you treat it. You don't win it over once and then live happily ever after. Time needs your attention. If you don't guard it, others try to steal it away.

Like a lover, if you disrespect it, you will be unhappy with the results.

On the other hand, the same way love grows with proper attention, so does time seemingly expand when you treat it with respect and affection. When you accept the bumps in the road of your relationship and focus forward, time, like a lover, can soften and become more cooperative and forgiving.

With both time and a lover, what you focus on increases. The Law of Attraction is at work everywhere! If you focus on how things aren't working out, you get more of things not working out. Instead, focus on what is working, what is positive and possible, and you receive more possibilities.

Like a lover—and like You—Time needs regular date nights and weekend escapes. A time when there is no demand on them other than to enjoy. A time when nothing needs to happen, just BE.

Unplugged

Personally, when life becomes crazy, I know it's time to take a personal day, unplugged. No phones, no computers, no TV, and no people. I put on headphones and listen to instrumental music (no distracting words).

During this time I keep a couple of notepads handy; invariably my mind wants to find something for me to "do." I write it down then let it go and return to just "being." Or I may do some inner-self work using one of the personal evolvement processes I've learned over the years (including some of the Time exercises I've learned in the past few years).

I call it my meditation day. People seem to have more respect for my downtime than if I say I'm going unplugged.

I always come away from the day not only with a renewed sense of peace but with insights and ideas to make my life or my business better, easier, more fun. I also come away with a renewed commitment to Self-care.

Speaking of Self-care…

Self-Care: Preparing Yourself for Your Lover

I don't know about you, but I appreciate when my lover takes care of himself—his health, his weight, the care he takes with his appearance. (Sorry guys. A slob never held much appeal.) A complaint many people seem to have, in an established relationship, is the

Time
is like a lover.
It responds
to the attention
you give it.

5th Truth of Time

other person lets themselves go. How can you inspire pride and affection unless you take pride in yourself?

Self-care isn't only about the physical appearance. It's taking the time to do what nurtures you. Dinner out with a girlfriend, an unplugged meditation day, sitting and reading your favorite book—these can all be nurturing activities.

One nurturing activity I've learned to enjoy my life coach suggested . It came in the form of dating advice: take time to prepare for a date, to move from the "doingness" of my day—a masculine energy—into my-receptive feminine.

After I started this practice, I enjoyed time with my lover more than when I quickly brushed my hair and threw on some lipstick. When I took the time to prepare, not only was I better prepared to enjoy, there was more of me present to give my lover some focused attention. Taking care of yourself is a path to happiness.

Time is like a lover. It appreciates when you take care of yourself.

Remember the Fifth Truth of Time:

> Time is like a lover. It responds to the attention you give it.

The Five Truths of Time—a Recap

Understanding the *Five Truths of Time* is the foundation of time-taming mastery.

1. Each day gives you 24 hours. It's yours to spend however you choose.
2. Time is for sale. You can buy more.
3. You can only have as much personal time as you take.
4. Time hides in the craziest places. Reclaim your time.
5. Time is like a lover. It responds to the attention you give it.

I think of these truths as time's secret treasures, because each secret shares how to enjoy more Time. What do you do with all this extra time? Have fun with it, of course!

Chapter 11

Next Steps

Pattern Change

Have you ever moved from a location you've been at for several years (a home, a job)? Did you ever find yourself leaving your house to go to work (or vice versa, if you changed jobs) and head to the old place automatically?

Your subconscious is a good thing. It keeps you from having to think things through every time you do them. Simple things like tying shoelaces or brushing your teeth before bed, to more complex activities like riding a bike or driving a car (especially a manual transmission, if you remember those).

But things can change and old skills (habits) don't apply. Take bicycling, for instance. Imaging being transported to a planet where bicycles gears require you to peddle backward to go forward. You would likely crash/fall over many times before you caught the hang of it.

Pattern-change is about changing an entrenched habit. It can be as awkward as learning a backward-geared bike. Taming Time puts you in a brand-new territory. It can feel awkward at times. Maybe next to impossible. But you can do it! You've chosen this new way of being because the old ways no longer serve you.

Muscle memory and mind patterns don't change with the flip of a switch. The easiest way to pattern-change is to practice. It's not something you can do once or twice a week and hope to master it. Like learning the weird backward-geared bicycle, you need to practice several times each week.

Simple Pattern-Change Tips

Pick one pattern you would like to change, then use these tips to support you in your adventure.

- First and foremost, be gentle with yourself.

- - How many years have you entrenched in this way of thinking or doing things? Beating yourself up won't help. Even babies take nine to sixteen months to learn to walk - and they don't have to unlearn old habits!
- Use each "crash" (life happens!) to make you even more determined to master your chosen path.
- Put the empowering processes on big sticky notes in the front of your journal.
  - Refer to them often
  - Move these forward as you complete one journal and begin the next
- Create an affirmation—a positive statement you repeat often to plant it deep in your subconscious.
  - Put your affirmation on sticky notes everywhere as a constant reminder
- Set a recurring daily alarm or text reminder displaying your affirmation.
  - Assign a unique notification or alarm tone. Make it fun! Try ringtone with a laughing baby or cackling witch.

Nothing can be done
from our past
except
to see it from a
new
perspective

Brendon Burchard

- Change the tone and time each week as a pattern interrupt.
- If you're the competitive type, keep score. Check in with yourself at the end of the day. Rate yourself on a scale of 1-5, where 5 means you lived the day operating from your new chosen style of being. Review last week's scores to see how you are improving.
  - If you score over 20 points, do something fun—even if it's just a happy dance around the living room shouting, "I'm awesome, I'm doing it!"
  - If you have a perfect score at the end of the week (6 days x 5 points/day = 30 points), do something extraordinary for yourself. You've earned it! Repeat and reward: do something "extraordinary" again.
- Give yourself a day off each week. No scoring, no beating yourself up.
- Whether or not you use the scoring system, give yourself a reward for your diligence.

If you haven't already read the chapter on mindset, do that now. Without the right mindset, changing your time pattern can look like a monster to conquer. It's so much more fun when you treat it like a game! Mindset is your magic wand.

It Takes a Village...

It takes a village. That phrase, attributed to an African proverb, holds so much truth.

In a village, there are elders to turn to—people with life experiences who have wisdom forged out of trials, failures, and successes. We all have wisdom and/or are growing into it, into a deeper understanding of what things work and what things make life more difficult than they need to be.

I remember the first time my Mom said to me, "How did you become so wise?" She was having problems with someone at work. I gave her a perspective on relating to others which shifted the situation for her. I didn't feel wise, but I was speaking from my experiences and what I had learned. We all have bits and pieces of wisdom tucked inside.

It takes a village. Sometimes by teaching another, we deepen the knowledge for ourselves. I remember Brenda from one of my mastermind groups. She complained her assistant had quit and now she had to find a new one. Several of the members murmured their sympathies—they had the same issue with finding good help. The hiring process—even for a part-time assistant—looked daunting.

I offered to host a class on the hiring tricks I had learned. They were delighted with the idea and the outcome. As I put my materials together and did additional research, I learned even more; it served me well the next time I hired someone.

It takes a village. A village is where you might find a best friend—the person you can call anytime you need someone to listen, someone to ask the right question so you can shift your perspective on a problem.

Every business owner needs a coach—or several! People they can turn to when they run into a roadblock. Someone who keeps them on course in a world full of rabbit holes.

No, this isn't a pitch for my services. (I take on very few private coaching clients.) But it is a call to action: to develop your support system, your support team. Personally, I have several different people I can turn to depending on my need at the moment: tax advisor, business strategy, mindset, social media, etc.

Business retreats are amazing villages. Yes, you can have more than one village. There I have met like-minded women walking the same path, dealing with the same struggles. There I have forged some of my best friendships. We are there to help and support each other.

Time to Thrive!

I've structured my business and *Time to Thrive*—both the village and the program—to provide education, hand-holding and community. A thriving village has all three.

I love to learn, and I love to share what I've learned. There is so much to share!

- Everything from mindset to these and other time-taming tricks
- Everything from hiring resources to marketing your business

It takes a village, and I invite you to join us in a space where you can both share your wisdom and learn from others.

Successful people say, to find the right answer; you have to ask the right question. I'm great at questions and excel at designing and implementing solutions. It's why Fortune 100 companies love me.

But my heart lies with the small businesses owner. You deserve a *fantastic* business. Start by doing the exercises in this book, taking advantage of our free Bonus (more details on the last page) and accepting the invitation to join our village.

Acknowledgments

This book would never have happened if it wasn't for the people who have supported my journey in the past few years. Without them, I would not be the person I am today—someone who is having more fun than ever and who has her arms around time (rather than time having a stranglehold on me).

I am blessed to have Therese Skelly, Jackie Simmons, Kayt Campbell, Tom Evans, LeeAnne Moody and Kate Harlow in my cheering section, sharing their love and wisdom.

Thank you, Barbara Grassey and Angela Lauria for your encouragement and practical advice in writing this book. Thank you Joyce Glass for your patience with my quibbles about grammar and voice; this book is better because of you.

Warren Godfrey, thank you for your creative talents, for designing a book cover I love, and for working through all the fine-tuning with me.

Mike Dooley and Jeanna Gabellini, thank you for being instrumental in upping my fun factor. (Jeanna, I knew business could be fun! You were the first person I heard who echoed that sentiment!)

Special thanks go to Kristine Velez. Kristine, without your help to transcribe my long-hand, scratchy writing, I never would have been able to publish this book.

It really does take a Village!

About the Author

As a solopreneur and business owner, Shauna has the first-hand experience of what overwhelm is like, to have to do more in one day than was possible to accomplish. She has felt the pain of marketing, hiring, payroll, and taxes.

She experienced the struggle of building a new business while continuing to work in a "day job" as a full-time solopreneur consultant to Fortune 100+ companies like Apple, PepsiCo, Tropicana, and ATT.

"It breaks my heart to see business owners floundering because they don't know the little tricks to create a business and their lives easier."

When Shauna hit burnout and could barely crawl out of bed, she knew something had to change. After 25 years as an independent consultant and business owner, she knew how to work hard, work long, and forget about fun. Now her health was on the line and relationships were non-existent.

It was a journey, but Shauna finally broke free and has more time, more fun, and a heartfelt business. She takes more time to read (she's an avid reader of everything from business and personal growth to murder mysteries and romance novels) and to travel.

Her favorite vacations include tropical beaches or visiting her son in Asheville, but there is a lot of the world Shauna still wants to see! Last year she took three weeks to travel to Scotland, England, and Italy with friends; it was her first "real" vacation since breaking free. "Why did I wait so long?" she asks. Now she prioritizes her vacation time.

Shauna loves to dance, learn new things, walk on the beach; drink fine wine and eat healthy food, and make a difference for business owners who are doing just fine, but want something more.

This book shares the magic Shauna found to shift from a 60+ hour work-week to a life and business style to allow more time, more fun, and the freedom to follow her passion.

Website: askShauna.com
Email: Shauna@askShauna.com
Facebook: facebook.com/askShauna

DISCLAIMER

Names and other details have been changed to respect my clients' privacy. Neither the author nor the publisher assumes any responsibility for errors, omissions, or contrary interpretations of the subject matter herein. Any perceived slight of any individual or organization is purely unintentional. Successes described are indicative of what's possible and do not infer a guarantee.

Brand and product names are trademarks or registered trademarks of their respective owners. Some links (not many) may be an affiliate link, which means I may be compensated (that would be fun!) if you use that link to purchase.

Free Bonus!

Because taming time, befriending it, is something that will happen over again in the face of new challenges, here are some free bonuses to help you along.

- *Ten Top Timesavers*, an e-book
- More Tools to Save you Time
  (Be sure to check out the video time-saver; it saves me hours every week.)
- A complete list of references and links from this book
- Recommended Books (some of my favs!)
- An invitation to join The Village
- Information about *Time to Thrive*

Get these and more at
    www.askShauna.com/Bonus
Access to your bonuses is 100% free.

> *Enjoy this book!*
>
> ## You are on the path to more Time, Money, and Fun.
>
> **Get the Bonus!**
>
> *Get your bonuses at askShauna.com/Bonus*

Thanks for reading! If you enjoyed this book or found it useful I'd be very grateful if you would post a short review on Amazon, or send me a note.

Your support really does make a difference! I read all the reviews personally so I can get your feedback and make the next book even better.

www.ingramcontent.com/pod-product-compliance
Lightning Source LLC
Chambersburg PA
CBHW060832050426
42453CB00008B/660